VENUS

GODDESS OF LOVE AND BEAUTY

by Teri Temple and Emily Temple
Illustrated by Eric Young

Gods and Goddesses of Ancient Rome

MEDIA ENHANCED BOOKS
AV2 BY WEIGL
ADDED VALUE · AUDIO VISUAL

www.av2books.com

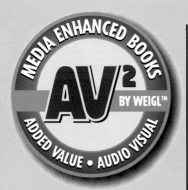

AV² provides enriched content that supplements and complements this book. Weigl's AV² books strive to create inspired learning and engage young minds in a total learning experience.

Your AV² Media Enhanced books come alive with...

Audio
Listen to sections of the book read aloud.

Key Words
Study vocabulary, and complete a matching word activity.

Video
Watch informative video clips.

Quizzes
Test your knowledge.

Go to **www.av2books.com**, and enter this book's unique code.

Embedded Weblinks
Gain additional information for research.

Slide Show
View images and captions, and prepare a presentation.

BOOK CODE

AVR74373

AV² **by Weigl** brings you media enhanced books that support active learning.

Try This!
Complete activities and hands-on experiments.

... and much, much more!

Published by AV² by Weigl
350 5th Avenue, 59th Floor
New York, NY 10118
Website: www.av2books.com

Printed in Brainerd, Minnesota, United States
1 2 3 4 5 6 7 8 9 0 22 21 20 19 18

102018
102318

Project Coordinator: Jared Siemens
Art Director: Terry Paulhus

Library of Congress Control Number: 2018961502

ISBN 978-1-4896-9519-2 (hardcover)
ISBN 978-1-4896-9520-8 (softcover)
ISBN 978-1-4896-9521-5 (multi-user eBook)

Weigl acknowledges Getty Images and Alamy as its primary image suppliers for this title.

Every reasonable effort has been made to trace ownership and to obtain permission to reprint copyright material. The publishers would be pleased to have any errors or omissions brought to their attention so that they may be corrected in subsequent printings.

CONTENTS

INTRODUCTION

In **ancient** times, Romans believed in spirits or gods called *numina*. In Latin, numina means "divine will" or "power." The Romans took part in religious rituals to please the gods. They felt the gods had powers that could make their lives better.

As the Roman government grew more powerful, its armies **conquered** many neighboring lands. Romans often adopted beliefs from these new cultures. They greatly admired the Greek arts and sciences. Gradually, the Romans combined the Greek myths and religion with their own. These stories shaped and influenced each part of a Roman citizen's daily life. Ancient Roman poets, such as Ovid and Virgil, wrote down these tales of wonder. Their writings became a part of Rome's great history. To the Romans, however, these stories were not just for entertainment. Roman mythology was their key to understanding the world.

ANCIENT ROMAN SOCIETIES

Ancient Roman society was divided into several groups. The patricians were the most powerful and wealthy group. They often owned land and held power in the government. The plebeians worked for the patricians. Slaves were prisoners of war or children without parents. Some slaves were freed and enjoyed most of the rights of citizens.

CHARACTERS AND PLACES

ANCIENT ROME

Adriatic Sea

● ROME

Tyrrhenian Sea

Cyprus
(SIGH-prus)
Island in the Mediterranean;
mythical home of Venus;
highest peak is Mount Olympus

Olympian Gods
(uh-LIM-pee-uhn / GAHDZ)
Ceres with daughter Proserpine, Mercury,
Vulcan, Venus with son Cupid, Mars,
Juno, Jupiter, Neptune, Minerva, Apollo,
Diana, Bacchus, Vesta, and Pluto

Mount Olympus
(MOWNT / uh-LIM-puhs)
The mountaintop home of the Olympian gods

Trojan War
(TROH-jin / WOHR)
War between the ancient
Greeks and Trojans

VENUS (VEE-nuhs)
Goddess of love and beauty; born of the sea
foam; wife of Vulcan; mother of Cupid

ADONIS (uh-DOH-nis)
Handsome Greek youth loved by Venus

AENEAS (ih-NEE-uhs)
Hero of the Trojan War; son of Anchises
and Venus; founder of Rome

ATALANTA (at-uh-LAN-tuh)
Greek heroine; agreed to marry only the
man who could beat her in a footrace

CAELUS (CEE-lus)
The sky and heavens; born of Terra along with
the mountains and seas; husband of Terra; father
of the Titans, Cyclopes, and Hecatoncheires

CUPID (KYOO-pid)
God of love; son of Venus; one of original
gods at beginning of creation

HELEN (HEL-uhn)
Daughter of Jupiter; her abduction
by Paris caused the Trojan War

JUPITER (JOO-pi-ter)
Supreme ruler of the heavens and of the gods who
lived on Mount Olympus; son of Saturn and Ops;
married to Juno; father of many gods and heroes

MARS (mahrz)
God of war; son of Jupiter and Juno;
possible father of Cupid

PARIS (PAR-is)
Trojan prince who caused the Trojan War
by kidnapping Helen of Sparta, Greece

PYGMALION (pig-MEY-lee-uhn)
Greek sculptor who fell in love with his statue

SATURN (SAT-ern)
A Titan who ruled the world; married to Ops; their
children became the first six Olympian gods

VULCAN (VULH-kuhn)
God of fire and metalwork; son of
Jupiter and Juno; married to Venus

THE GODDESS OF LOVE AND BEAUTY

O f all the gods in the **Pantheon**, Venus's story is unique. While most other gods descended from two parents, Venus did not. Her story begins not long after the creation of the universe.

Only Chaos existed before the universe was created. Mother Earth, or Terra, rose out of Chaos to create the heavens and Earth. Terra gave birth to Caelus. He was the father of the heavens and the sky. Terra and Caelus had many children together. Caelus thought his children were ugly and feared they would try to take his power. He locked them deep in the **underworld**. Caelus's actions made Terra sad. Terra convinced her son, Saturn, to help her defeat Caelus. Saturn took a special sickle and attacked his father. Saturn cut off parts of Caelus's body and tossed them into the sea. These body parts mixed with the foam of the sea and created Venus. She was stunningly beautiful. As a result, she became the goddess of love and beauty.

PLANET VENUS

Venus was one of the Roman goddesses whose name was given to a planet. Her planet is the brightest object in the sky. It can often be seen in the daylight. Venus is the closest planet to Earth. It is sometimes called Earth's "twin" because it is similar in size. Ancient Romans and Greeks thought the planet Venus was two star gods: Vesper, which meant "evening star," and Lucifer, or "light bringer."

Venus rose out of the sea foam on a big seashell. She was alone except for the West Wind, named Favonius. Favonius blew Venus gently through the waves of the sea. Eventually, Venus landed on the island of Cyprus. On the island, the Horae greeted Venus. They represented the seasons. Venus grew to be a great beauty. When she was fully grown, it was time for her to leave Cyprus. The Horae dressed her in beautiful clothes adorned with jewels and precious gems. A crown of violets rested on her golden hair.

When Venus arrived at Mount Olympus, the other gods saw her beauty. It took their breath away. The gods welcomed Venus. They gave her a golden **throne**. She would rule over love and beauty. Venus took her place among the gods and goddesses at Mount Olympus.

DEI CONSENTES

There were 12 gods and goddesses who made up the Dei Consentes. There were six powerful gods: Jupiter, Mars, Neptune, Vulcan, Apollo, and Mercury. There were also six majestic goddesses: Juno, Minerva, Vesta, Ceres, Diana, and Venus. The people of Rome believed the gods lived together on Mount Olympus. Romans prayed to the gods to help defeat Roman enemies.

Not long after Venus arrived on Mount Olympus, the other goddesses became jealous. The gods admired Venus because she was so beautiful.

Vulcan was one of the many gods who loved Venus. However, Vulcan was born **deformed** and ugly. He thought because of his looks Venus would never love him back. Vulcan's mother was Juno, the queen goddess. She had treated Vulcan poorly when he was young. Vulcan was still angry with his mother. He decided to get revenge on his mother and win Venus's love at the same time. Vulcan was a skilled craftsman and **blacksmith**. He built Juno a glorious throne. Juno loved it and sat down right away. But when she did, the throne trapped her. None of the gods could figure out how to get Juno out. She and the other gods begged Vulcan to let her go. He refused.

Juno promised Venus as a bride to whoever could release her. Venus was stunned. She wanted Mars, the god of war, as her husband. Mars tried, but he could not release Juno. Eventually Vulcan freed Juno. He took Venus as his bride. This made Venus very unhappy.

The most famous throne in the world has been used by 38 kings and queens of Great Britain and is called the Coronation Chair. The chair was built in the 13th century and is located at Westminster Abbey.

Even though Vulcan had tricked Venus into marriage, he still wanted her to be happy. He loved her. Seeing Venus unhappy made Vulcan sad, too. He decided to cheer her up by making her a special gift. Vulcan used his skills to make Venus a magic girdle. The girdle would make all men fall hopelessly in love with her. The magic of the girdle made Venus completely irresistible.

Venus loved Mars. She decided to use her magic girdle to try to win his affection. Mars and Venus began to meet in secret. Sol, the Sun god, caught them sneaking around. He told Vulcan. Vulcan was extremely angry. He crafted a magic net to trap them. Then he had Sol watch for Mars and Venus.

The next time Mars and Venus were together, Sol waited until they fell asleep to throw the net over them. The net ensnared their bodies. Vulcan hoped Mars would be embarrassed by the affair and stop seeing Venus. But it wasn't all Mars's fault. He was just another god helpless against Venus's powerful beauty.

SOL

Sol was the Roman god of the Sun. He was similar to the Greek god Helios. According to legend, Sol had a very important job. He was to ride a golden chariot across the sky each morning and bring in the dawn. Four fire-breathing horses pulled his chariot. At the end of the day, he rode into the west so he could sleep. Sol's position in the sky allowed him to see all that happened below. He often caught gods in their tricks and dishonesty.

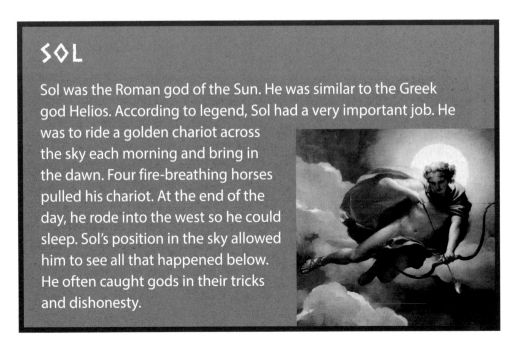

As the goddess of love, Venus had many love affairs. She had great powers over men and gods alike. The Olympian gods Bacchus, Mercury, and Neptune also fell under Venus's spell. These relationships produced many children. However, she had the most children with Mars. Some legends say they had four children. Other stories say they had five children.

The first child Venus and Mars had was Concordia. She was lovely like her mother and also gentle. Concordia **personified** peace and harmony. Next, Mars and Venus had a set of twins. Their twins were named Timor and Metus. They were like their father. They became the gods of fear and terror. Timor and Metus followed their father into war and onto battlefields. Mars and Venus's last child took after Venus. He was a god of love. His name was Cupid. Cupid was the most mischievous child.

Venus had many powerful children, but she was also powerful herself. Venus had the ability to make any pair of people fall in love. She used her powers on the gods. But she also liked to help humans fall in love. This sometimes had disastrous results.

In ancient Rome, Venus was celebrated during the month of April because she represents new life. The festivals in April celebrated love and the grape harvest.

The Roman myths describe Venus as beautiful. However, they noted that her beauty made her conceited. Her job on Mount Olympus was to organize the social gatherings of the gods. She decorated the social hall for events with her favorite things. Venus loved swans, doves, roses, apples, and seashells.

Venus had attendants who helped her with her duties. They were called the Gratiae, better known as the Graces. The Graces were sister goddesses. They danced through Olympus, entertaining the gods. The Graces also helped Venus by blessing young women with beauty, charm, and goodness. Youthful winged gods called the Amores also accompanied Venus. They were named Himerus, Anteros, and Pothos. They made Venus's powers stronger.

WOMEN IN ANCIENT ROME

The role of women in ancient Rome was very different from the role of women in society today. The government did not recognize women, children, or slaves as citizens. As wives, women stayed home and ran the household. They were responsible for taking care of the family. When Rome became an empire, women gained some power in society.

Venus's son, Cupid, was always with her. His job was to help Venus
with her dealings in love. Cupid carried a bow and special arrows.
He could shoot his arrows at people or gods to make them fall in love
with each other. However, his arrows could also produce feelings of
indifference or hatred.

There were many famous lovers in ancient mythology. Venus was responsible for bringing many of the couples together. Perhaps the most well-known pair was Paris and Helen. The legend began with all of the goddesses receiving an invitation to a wedding on Mount Olympus. Discordia was the only goddess not invited. She was the goddess of **discord**.

As such, she responded to the insult by creating a problem. She placed a golden apple on the banquet table at the wedding. The apple had an inscription that read, "For the fairest." When the goddesses arrived, the apple caused quite a stir. The goddesses began to argue about who was the most beautiful. They decided the most handsome man in the world should be the judge.

VENUS IN ART

Though their myths are often similar, the ancient Greeks and Romans differed when it came to art. The Greeks made their drawings or sculptures of absolutely perfect people. Roman art contained people who had flaws. Both Greeks and Romans frequently used Venus as the subject of their art. There are many famous statues and paintings of Venus throughout history. One famous mosaic is *The Judgement of Paris*. The art shows Venus sitting on a rock.

This man was Paris, a youthful Trojan prince. In order to win his favor, the goddesses began to offer him prizes. Juno, the queen of the gods, said she would give Paris power. Athena, the goddess of war, promised to help Paris win his battles. Venus thought Paris might want the love of the most beautiful woman in the world more than power or victory. She promised to give him Helen as his wife.

GODS AND GODDESSES OF ANCIENT ROME

Paris quickly called Venus the fairest and gave her the golden apple. He then traveled to Greece, where Helen lived. When Paris arrived, Helen fell in love with him immediately. Helen willingly left Greece with Paris. Venus promised to help them elope. There was one small problem—Helen was already married to the Greek king Menelaus. Menelaus was furious when he saw his wife had been kidnapped. He put together the greatest Greek army ever assembled to help get her back.

A war began between the Greeks and Paris's Trojans. The Trojan War became a legendary battle in ancient Greek and Roman history. The battle lasted 10 years. In the end, it looked like Greece was going to surrender. They left a giant wooden horse outside of the Trojans' camp. The Trojans thought it was a gift. They brought the hollowed horse inside their camp. As soon as it was within the gates, Greek soldiers leapt out of the horse. The Greeks opened the camp gates and let in more soldiers. They killed all of the Trojan soldiers and took over Troy. Paris was killed in the battle, and Helen had to go back to her husband.

In 1870, a German archaeologist found evidence of a war at the ancient city of Troy. The story of the Trojan War may have been inspired by a real war that happened around 1180 BC.

Even before the Trojan War, the gods were tired of Venus's games. Jupiter decided to play a trick on her. He crafted a love spell that would make her fall in love with a man named Anchises. He was a handsome member of the Trojan royal family. Venus had a baby with him, named Aeneas. She swore Anchises to secrecy, but Anchises failed. When he revealed the name of his son's mother, Anchises was killed by Jupiter's thunderbolt.

Aeneas went on to become a leader in the Trojan army. Because he was the son of Venus, she and other gods often protected him on the battlefield. One myth says Venus helped Aeneas escape when Troy fell to the Greeks. After fleeing the city, Venus made the queen of Carthage, Dido, fall in love with Aeneas. Dido offered to keep him safe in her city. Legend says Aeneas led a group of **refugees** to Italy and eventually founded the city of Rome. When Aeneas died, Venus convinced Jupiter to make Aeneas a god.

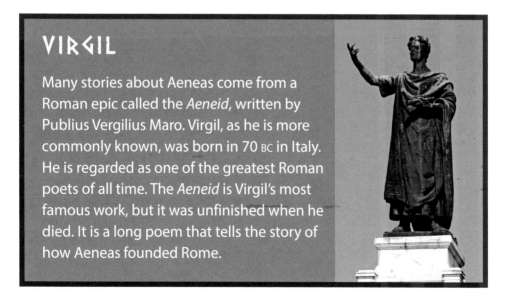

VIRGIL

Many stories about Aeneas come from a Roman epic called the *Aeneid*, written by Publius Vergilius Maro. Virgil, as he is more commonly known, was born in 70 BC in Italy. He is regarded as one of the greatest Roman poets of all time. The *Aeneid* is Virgil's most famous work, but it was unfinished when he died. It is a long poem that tells the story of how Aeneas founded Rome.

Not all of Venus's endeavors ended so well. Venus thought Adonis was so beautiful as a baby that she kept him for herself. She locked him in a chest and gave him to Proserpine in the underworld. Proserpine opened the box and was equally taken with Adonis's beauty. When Venus came back for him, Proserpine refused to give him up. Jupiter solved the problem by saying Adonis would spend time with each goddess. This made Mars upset. He killed Adonis. After Adonis was dead, Venus mourned for many years.

Though Venus was mischievous, she created as many perfect matches as she did problems in love. One success story was that of Pygmalion, a sculptor in ancient Greece. He made an ivory sculpture of a beautiful woman named Galatea. Then he asked Venus for a wife who was as beautiful as the sculpture. Venus turned the statue into a real woman. Galatea and Pygmalion fell deeply in love.

Hippomenes was in love with Atalanta. She was a maiden who was a speedy runner. Atalanta said she would marry the man who beat her in a race. Hippomenes knew he could not outrun her, so he asked Venus for help. Venus gave him golden apples to distract Atalanta. When Atalanta stopped to pick up the apples, Hippomenes gained enough time to win the race and earn her as his bride.

Venus's rise to importance among the Roman gods is somewhat of a mystery. Before she was known as the goddess of love, ancient Italians worshipped Venus as a goddess of gardens and vineyards. She had no myths of her own until the Roman religion blended its stories with the Greek myths. Ancient Italians began to relate her to Aphrodite, the goddess of love.

Cyprus was considered Venus's mythical home since it was where she grew up. However, not all of the myths agree that Venus was created from Caelus's parts mixing with sea foam. Some say instead that her parents were Jupiter and Dione.

THE TEMPLE OF VENUS

A temple dedicated to Venus is located in the city of Rome. An emperor named Hadrian designed the Temple of Venus. It was completed and dedicated in 135 AD. The Temple of Venus was once the largest temple in the ancient city.

However, it was damaged twice, so only a few columns remain. Ancient Romans used the temple as a place to worship the goddess in hopes of good fortune and longevity for Rome.

Venus became more important to the Romans because of Julius Caesar and his family. They claimed that one of Aeneas's sons was their ancestor. If that were true, it would mean they were descendants of Venus as well. Ancient Romans honored Venus in April by holding two important festivals in her name, Veneralia and Vinalia Rustica.

Regardless of how Venus became prominent in Roman mythology, she has long been one of the most important goddesses. She will always be remembered for her beauty and will continue inspiring stories of love.

PRINCIPAL GODS OF ROMAN MYTHOLOGY— A FAMILY TREE

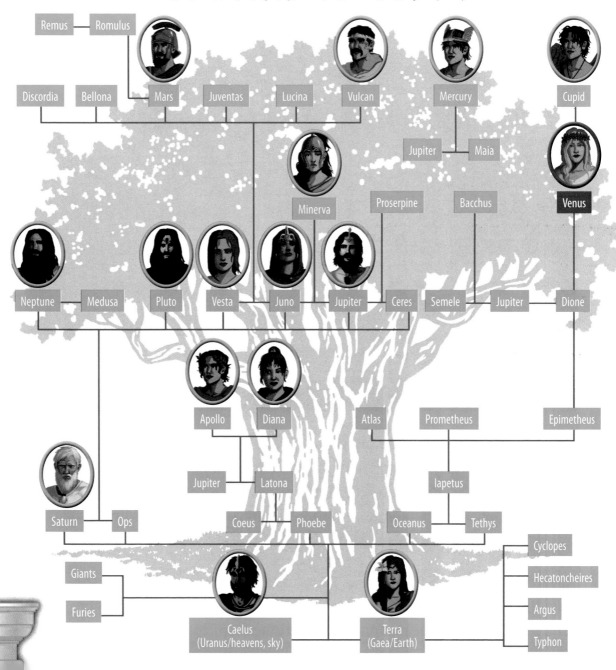

KEY WORDS

ancient: from the very distant past

blacksmith: a person who works with iron

conquered: took control of through military force

deformed: misshapen or abnormal in shape, often of a body part

discord: disagreement

Pantheon: the entire group of gods and goddesses from a certain religion

personified: to represent or embody a specific idea in physical form

refugees: people forced to leave their country to escape war or a natural disaster

throne: a chair used for special occasions for royalty

underworld: home of the dead

INDEX

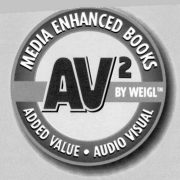

Log on to www.av2books.com

AV² by Weigl brings you media enhanced books that support active learning. Go to www.av2books.com, and enter the special code found on page 2 of this book. You will gain access to enriched and enhanced content that supplements and complements this book. Content includes video, audio, weblinks, quizzes, a slide show, and activities.

AV² Online Navigation

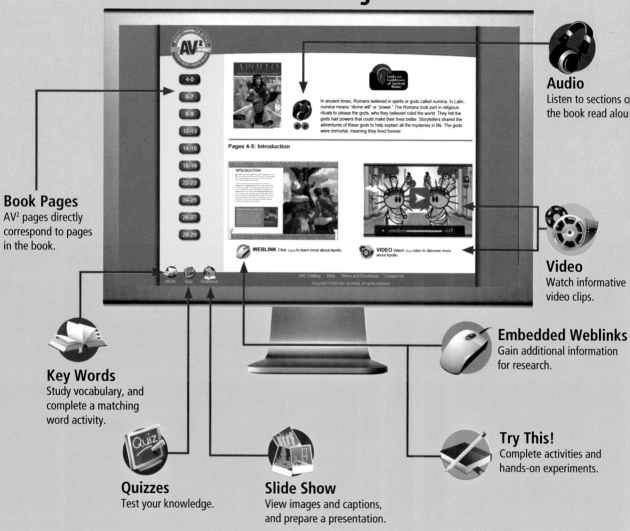

Audio
Listen to sections of the book read aloud

Book Pages
AV² pages directly correspond to pages in the book.

Video
Watch informative video clips.

Embedded Weblinks
Gain additional information for research.

Key Words
Study vocabulary, and complete a matching word activity.

Try This!
Complete activities and hands-on experiments.

Quizzes
Test your knowledge.

Slide Show
View images and captions, and prepare a presentation.

AV² was built to bridge the gap between print and digital. We encourage you to tell us what you like and what you want to see in the future.

Sign up to be an AV² Ambassador at www.av2books.com/ambassador.